D0759897

CUTE AND UNUSUAL PETS

SUGAR GLIDERS

by Paula Wilson

Consultant
Sarrah Kaye
Veterinarian and General Curator
Staten Island Zoo
Staten Island, New York

CAPSTONE PRESS
a capstone imprint

Snap Books are published by Capstone Press,
1710 Roe Crest Drive, North Mankato, Minnesota 56003
www.mycapstone.com

Library of Congress Cataloging-in-Publication Data
Names: Wilson, Paula M., 1963- author.
Title: Sugar gliders / by Paula M. Wilson.
Description: North Mankato, Minnesota : an imprint of Capstone Press, [2019]
   | Series: Snap books. Cute and unusual pets. | Audience: Age 8-14.
Identifiers: LCCN 2018016130 (print) | LCCN 2018017760 (ebook) |
   ISBN 9781543530667 (eBook PDF) |
   ISBN 9781543530575 (hardcover)
Subjects: LCSH: Sugar gliders—Juvenile literature.
Classification: LCC SF459.S83 (ebook) | LCC SF459.S83 W55 2019 (print) | DDC
   636.92—dc23
LC record available at https://lccn.loc.gov/2018016130

Editorial Credits
Lauren Dupuis-Perez, editor
Sara Radka, designer
Kathy McColley, production specialist

Image Credits
Getty Images: eugenesergeev, 11, TracyCarb, 21; Shutterstock: bluedog studio, 24, Evannovostro, 14, Kamonrat, 12, 17, 25, kamui29, 23, Land_bun, 8, maruchit phonsuriphat, 19, Monkeyoum, 5, 27, 28, Napat, cover, Oleg Blazhyievskyi, 7 (bottom), pandpstock001, back cover, 29, Ploychan Lompong, 13, Praisaeng, 15, 26, Ratana Prongjai, 1, TaaPu, 7 (top)

Glossary terms are bolded on first use in text.

TABLE OF CONTENTS

CHAPTER 1
MEET THE SUGAR GLIDER

What's that cute animal with big, round eyes? It's a sugar glider! Sugar gliders are friendly, curious, and playful. They make great pets for the right household. These adorable, furry animals form lifelong bonds with their owners and other sugar gliders.

Sugar gliders are about the size of chipmunks. However, they are not related to chipmunks or other **rodents**. In fact, they belong to the possum family. Sugar gliders are **marsupials**, like kangaroos and koala bears. Female marsupials have pouches to carry their young.

The word "sugar" in its name comes from the animal's favorite foods—plant nectar and sugary tree sap. It gets the second part of its name from its ability to glide high among the tree branches. Sugar gliders can glide up to 150 feet (46 meters). That is half the length of a football field.

---

rodent—a mammal with long front teeth used for gnawing; rats, mice, and squirrels are rodents

marsupial—an animal that carries its young in a pouch

DID YOU KNOW?

The Latin name for a sugar glider is *Petaurus breviceps.* This means "short-headed rope dancer."

5

SUGAR GLIDERS IN THE WILD

Sugar gliders are **native** to the forests of Australia, Indonesia, and New Guinea. They are arboreal. This means they spend most of their time in trees, not on the ground. These small animals build nests in hollow trees using leaves and twigs. Eucalyptus trees are a favorite spot for them to call home. Up in the trees, **predators** are less likely to find them.

Sugar gliders eat mostly plant nectar, tree sap, and insects. They live in small groups called colonies. In each colony, one or two males are **dominant**. The males use scent glands on their heads and feet to mark the other members of their colony. They also mark the area where the colony lives. Other sugar gliders know to keep out.

DID YOU KNOW?

When a sugar glider is born, it is about the size of a grain of rice and has no hair.

native—growing or living naturally in a particular place
predator—an animal that hunts other animals for food
dominant—very powerful or important

As soon as a sugar glider is born, it moves into its mother's pouch. The baby, called a joey, stays in the pouch for about 70 days. Then it spends about two months in a nest until it can survive without its mother or father. Male sugar gliders are active in taking care of the young. They help keep the joeys warm and look after them.

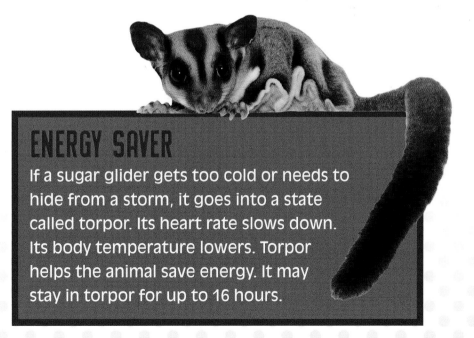

ENERGY SAVER

If a sugar glider gets too cold or needs to hide from a storm, it goes into a state called torpor. Its heart rate slows down. Its body temperature lowers. Torpor helps the animal save energy. It may stay in torpor for up to 16 hours.

PHYSICAL FEATURES

Sugar gliders are **nocturnal**. This means they are more active at night. Their big round eyes help them see in the dark.

A flap of skin connects a sugar glider's front feet to its back feet. This flap is called a patagium. The patagium acts like a parachute as the animal glides. Its long tail helps it steer. A sugar glider's tail is partly **prehensile**. It lets the animal grip leaves and brush.

DID YOU KNOW?

The ankle joints of sugar gliders rotate 180 degrees. This allows them to climb down a tree headfirst.

Sugar gliders have very good night vision, but they only see in shades of gray and red.

GLIDING HIGH

Sugar gliders might look like they are flying, but they are actually gliding through the air. Unlike birds, sugar gliders do not have wings to flap. Sugar gliders launch themselves from one branch and grab onto the next with all four feet.

Sugar gliders have five toes on each foot. Sharp claws help them hang onto tree branches. Like humans, they have **opposable thumbs**. These thumbs help sugar gliders grip tree branches and pick up food.

Most sugar gliders are gray. A dark stripe runs down their backs. Their faces are also striped. Cream-colored fur covers their underbellies. Some sugar gliders are white or tan. A sugar glider is 5 to 7 inches (13 to 18 centimeters) long. Its tail is 6 to 10 inches (15 to 25 cm) long. An adult sugar glider weighs 3 to 5 ounces (85 to 142 grams).

---

nocturnal—active at night and resting during the day
prehensile—capable of grasping, especially around something
opposable thumb—a thumb that can be moved around to touch the other fingers; animals with opposable thumbs can grasp and pick up things

CHAPTER 2
SUGAR GLIDERS AS PETS

Sugar gliders are somewhat new to the pet world. People first began keeping them as pets in the 1990s, mostly in the United States and Canada. Their tiny bodies and adorable faces make them hard to resist. Sugar gliders make great companions. They are social animals. They like to be with their owners and other sugar gliders. Another reason they are such popular pets is that they do not have strong odors. Sugar gliders groom themselves. They only need occasional bathing.

Social media has helped sugar gliders become more well-known in recent years. Dozens of Facebook groups are dedicated to sugar gliders and their owners. Instagram and Twitter feature hundreds of photos of this pet. A pair of sugar gliders named Jimjim and Jumpee have 20,000 followers on Instagram. Another Instagram account called Sugar Glider Nation has nearly 30,000 followers.

Some owners walk around their homes with their sugar gliders in their pockets.

GLIDER CON

Gliding Together is a sugar glider conference held every year in Ohio. The conference brings together sugar glider owners from around the country. They go to workshops and have discussions with experts. The conference also gives owners the chance to show off their pets.

ARE SUGAR GLIDERS IN YOUR FUTURE?

Caring for a pet is a big responsibility. Sugar gliders need daily attention from their owners. Talk to your parents about owning a sugar glider. Answer these questions before you decide if a sugar glider is right for you:

• Do you have the time to care for a sugar glider, including feeding, cleaning the cage, and playing with it?

• Who will take care of your sugar glider? You or your parents or siblings?

- Sugar gliders are happier and healthier around other sugar gliders. Are you and your family OK with owning more than one?

- How much do sugar gliders cost to buy and feed? Who will take on those costs? You or your parents?

- Do the veterinarians in your area take care of sugar gliders?

- Do you have space in your home for a sugar glider cage?

- Do you have other pets, such as a cat or a dog? Will these animals get along with a sugar glider?

Learn as much as you can about sugar gliders before deciding if they are right for you and your family.

MORE TO KNOW

Do you want a sugar glider and think you are ready for the responsibility? You will first need to consider a few more things. Sugar gliders are social animals. Their **instinct** is to bond with others. If a sugar glider does not receive enough attention, it can develop depression or other health issues. For this reason **breeders** strongly recommend buying more than one sugar glider. In fact, some breeders will not sell a single sugar glider. When buying two sugar gliders, a **neutered** male and a female is a good combination. Do not try to breed your own sugar gliders. Only licensed breeders can breed them.

Even though sugar gliders are small, they still need attention every day.

You will also need to make sure sugar gliders are allowed as pets where you live. Some places, including Alaska, California, Hawaii, and New York City, have laws against owning sugar gliders. The laws are in place to prevent owners from releasing unwanted sugar gliders into the wild. Freed sugar gliders compete with native animals for food and living space. They also do not have the skills to survive in the wild. If you get a sugar glider but then decide it is not the right pet for you, do not release it into the wild. Find a home for it with a breeder or with someone who wants to adopt it.

---

instinct—behavior that is natural rather than learned
breeder—a person who raises animals to sell
neuter—to operate on a male animal so it is unable to produce young

WHICH PET TO GET

Where should you get your pet sugar gliders? One option is to buy them from a breeder. Be sure to find a breeder who is licensed to sell the animals. A breeder will help you choose your sugar gliders. He or she will also show you how to take care of them. Plan to pay $200 to $1,000 for each animal. Rescuing a sugar glider from a shelter is another option. Check with your local animal shelter to see if it has any sugar gliders that need a home.

Choose sugar gliders that are healthy and have good **temperaments**. A sugar glider's eyes should be black and clear. Its tail should be full and bushy. Its coat should be smooth and soft. A sugar glider should be at least 8 weeks old before you bring it home. At this age, a sugar glider can **adapt** to its new surroundings. A sugar glider is fully grown by age 1.

---

temperament—the combination of an animal's behavior and personality; the way an animal usually acts or responds to situations shows its temperament
adapt—to change to fit into a new or different environment

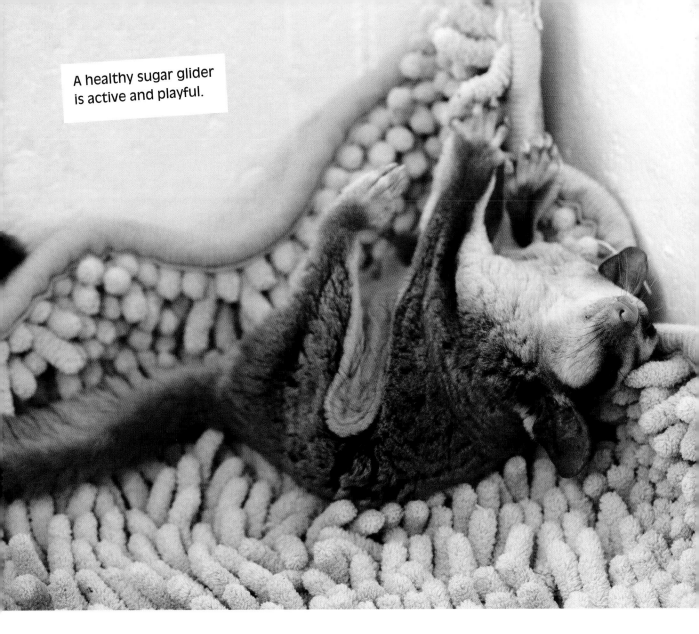

VISIT THE VET

After you bring home your sugar gliders, make an appointment with a vet who knows how to take care of the animals. The vet will make sure your sugar gliders are healthy. He or she can also give you advice on feeding and caring for your new companion. Visit the vet once a year to check your pet's weight and overall health.

CHAPTER 3
CARING FOR SUGAR GLIDERS

Before you bring home your sugar gliders, make sure you have the right cage. Find a tall wire cage with good air flow. Sugar gliders need room to glide around inside. A cage that is at least 36 inches (91 cm) tall and 24 inches (61 cm) wide gives them enough room to move. Sugar gliders can squeeze through very tiny spaces. Make sure the cage's wires are spaced no more than a 0.5 inch (1 cm) apart. Line the bottom of the cage with soft bedding from your local pet store.

Once you have the right cage, make sure your sugar gliders stay happy inside. Sugar gliders like to sleep snuggled in an enclosed area. Get a nesting box or a mini sleeping bag for each animal. Sugar gliders need to stay active and get enough exercise. An exercise wheel is a must. You can also create different levels in the cage. Your sugar gliders will move from one level to the next.

It is important to keep your sugar gliders' cage clean.

Clean your sugar gliders' cage regularly. Wipe it down and remove droppings and leftover food each day. Clean the rest of the cage once a week. At this time change the bedding. Also wash any fabric items, such as sleeping bags.

FOOD AND NUTRITION

Sugar gliders need the right foods and enough water to stay healthy. Attach a bottle to their cage and keep it filled with fresh, clean water. Purchase food pellets made for sugar gliders. Many owners mix fresh food for their pets. This includes hard-boiled eggs, honey, yogurt, fruits, and vegetables. Feeding sugar gliders different foods gives them many nutrients. It also lets them experience different textures. Mealworms, crickets, and dried fruit make great treats. Sugar gliders do not always get enough calcium. You may need to add a liquid vitamin to their diet.

CLEAN AND CLIPPED

Sugar gliders groom themselves. They do not need to be bathed often. Ask your breeder or pet store about shampoo for sugar gliders. The shampoo should not dry out their skin.

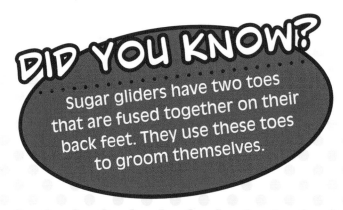

DID YOU KNOW?
Sugar gliders have two toes that are fused together on their back feet. They use these toes to groom themselves.

Sugar gliders have very sharp nails. You can cut their nails with small nail clippers. Be sure you do not cut off too much. Sugar gliders need their nails to grip when they jump and glide. Be careful not to cut too deeply. It is easy to clip down into the soft part of the nail and cause bleeding.

A vet can show you how to trim sugar glider nails.

CHAPTER 4
LIFE WITH SUGAR GLIDERS

Start the bonding process as soon as you get a new sugar glider. This process takes patience and time. Your goal is to gain your sugar glider's trust. You also want the animal to get used to your voice and smell. Start slowly by talking to your pet. A sugar glider will probably be scared at first. Let it get used to its cage for the first few days before you pet it.

Some owners wear a holder called a bonding pouch. The pouch is a great way for a sugar glider to get used to your scent and voice. Other family members should also wear the pouch so each sugar glider becomes familiar with them as well. The pouch also keeps a sugar glider warm and cozy.

Breeders recommend creating a schedule when you first bring your sugar glider home. Make a chart that records when you take your pet out of the cage and for how long. You can also track its feeding times and what it eats.

Spending time with your sugar gliders is the best way to form a lasting bond.

SAMPLE SUGAR GLIDER CARE CHART

Date	Out of Cage	In Cage	Time Fed	Type of Food
3/20	2:30PM	3:30PM	4:00PM	VEGETABLES
3/21	1:15PM	2:15PM	3:30PM	YOGURT
3/22	3:00PM	4:00PM	4:30PM	EGGS
3/23	1:00PM	3:30PM	4:00PM	CRICKETS

The best time to interact with your sugar gliders is when they are awake and alert.

YOUR SIDEKICK

Daily interaction with sugar gliders should not stop after they have grown to adulthood. They thrive on your attention. Carry your sugar gliders in a pouch while you are doing chores, reading, or watching television. Although sugar gliders are nocturnal, they can adjust somewhat to your schedule. Sugar gliders can be alert and active in the late afternoon or evening.

Sugar gliders are noisy animals. Knowing what the noises mean will help you understand more about your pet. Sugar gliders hiss when they are grooming themselves. They purr when they are content. They make a barking sound when they want your attention.

ADDING TO THE FAMILY

You may decide to get another sugar glider later. Start the bonding process the same way you did with your first sugar gliders. Keep the new sugar glider in a separate cage and let it get to know your other sugar gliders slowly. Have them spend a few minutes together each day. Eventually, they will become familiar with each other and may be able live in the same cage.

HAPPY GLIDERS

Keeping sugar gliders happy is easy, especially if you give them different ways to stay active. Sugar gliders love to jump and climb. Add tree branches, rope ladders, and ledges to their cages for them to explore. Toys used for pet birds, such as bells, swings, and hanging balls, also work well for this pet. Setting up ledges high in the cage gives your sugar gliders a place to sit and jump from. Sugar gliders also enjoy quiet time. They are likely happy curled up in a bonding pouch against your chest.

KEEPING THEM SAFE

Do not let your sugar gliders roam freely around your home. They can fit into tiny places, such as vents and under

the refrigerator. They might get stuck or injured. Be careful if you take your sugar gliders outside. They could get loose and have trouble finding their way back to you. Other animals may harm sugar gliders as well.

Sugar gliders are happiest when they are active. A wheel inside a glider's cage will help keep them healthy.

Try these safe ways to let your sugar gliders spend time out of their cage. Some breeders suggest setting up a small tent with enough room for you and your sugar gliders to move around. Other owners create a room in their house that is safe for sugar gliders to roam and explore. Pet sugar gliders will enjoy being able to glide from one area to another.

Your entire family should get to know and enjoy these playful pets.

MEMBERS OF THE FAMILY

Sugar gliders are cute and lovable animals. If you and your family are ready for the commitment, sugar gliders can be rewarding pets. By spending time with your sugar gliders every day, you will form a special bond with them.

Take the time to learn all about sugar gliders. Read more books about them and have a parent help you research the animals online. Consider joining a sugar glider club and get to know other owners. The more you learn about these unique animals, the better you can care for them. Pet sugar gliders can live for 12 to 15 years. By taking good care of your pets, you can enjoy many years together.

GLOSSARY

adapt (uh-DAPT)—to change to fit into a new or different environment

breeder (BREE-der)—a person who raises animals to sell

dominant (DOM-uh-nuh-nt)—very powerful or important

instinct (IN-stingkt)—behavior that is natural rather than learned

marsupial (mahr-SOO-pee-uhl)—an animal that carries its young in a pouch

native (NAY-tiv)—growing or living naturally in a particular place

neuter (NOO-tur)—to operate on a male animal so it is unable to produce young

nocturnal (nok-TUR-nuhl)—active at night and resting during the day

opposable thumb (uh-POH-zuh-buhl THUHM)—a thumb that can be moved around to touch the other fingers; animals with opposable thumbs can grasp and pick up things

predator (PRED-uh-tur)—an animal that hunts other animals for food

prehensile (pree-HEN-sahyl)—capable of grasping, especially around something

rodent (ROHD-uhnt)—a mammal with long front teeth used for gnawing; rats, mice, and squirrels are rodents

temperament (TEM-pur-uh-muhnt)—the combination of an animal's behavior and personality; the way an animal usually acts or responds to situations shows its temperament

READ MORE

Collard III, Sneed B. *Catching Air: Taking the Leap with Gliding Animals.* How Nature Works. Thomaston, Maine: Tilbury House Publishers, 2017.

Cronin, Leonard. *The Australian Animal Atlas.* Crows Nest, Australia: Allen and Unwin, 2017.

Kenney, Karen Latchana. *Sugar Glider.* You Have a Pet What?! Vero Beach, Fla: Rourke Educational Media, 2015.

Wightman, Caroline. *Sugar Gliders.* Hauppauge, N.Y.: Barron's, 2016.

INTERNET SITES

Use FactHound to find Internet sites related to this book.

Visit *www.facthound.com*

Just type in 9781543530575 and go.

Check out projects, games and lots more at
www.capstonekids.com

INDEX